The Metropolitan Museum of Art

MUSEUMS OF THE WORLD

By Joy Gregory

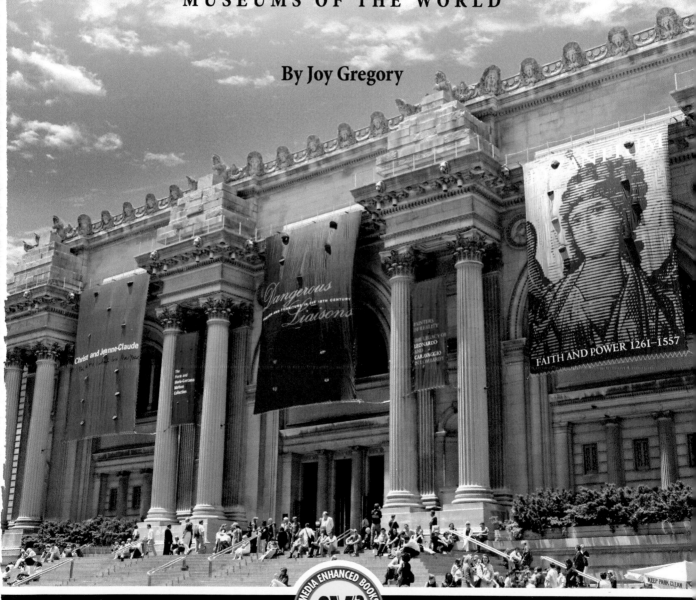

MEDIA ENHANCED BOOKS
AV2 BY WEIGL
ADDED VALUE · AUDIO VISUAL
www.av2books.com

AV² provides enriched content that supplements and complements this book. Weigl's AV² books strive to create inspired learning and engage young minds in a total learning experience.

Your AV² Media Enhanced books come alive with...

Audio
Listen to sections of the book read aloud.

Video
Watch informative video clips.

Embedded Weblinks
Gain additional information for research.

Try This!
Complete activities and hands-on experiments.

Key Words
Study vocabulary, and complete a matching word activity.

Quizzes
Test your knowledge.

Slide Show
View images and captions, and prepare a presentation.

... and much, much more!

Go to www.av2books.com, and enter this book's unique code.

BOOK CODE

S481600

AV² **by Weigl** brings you media enhanced books that support active learning.

Published by AV² by Weigl
350 5th Avenue, 59th Floor
New York, NY 10118
Websites: www.av2books.com www.weigl.com

Copyright ©2015 AV² by Weigl

Library of Congress Cataloging-in-Publication Data
Gregory, Joy (Joy Marie)
The Metropolitan Museum of Art / Joy Gregory.
   pages cm. -- (Museums of the world)
Includes index.
ISBN 978-1-4896-1194-9 (hardcover : alk. paper) — ISBN 978-1-4896-1195-6 (softcover : alk. paper)
— ISBN 978-1-4896-1196-3 (single user ebk.) — ISBN 978-1-4896-1197-0 (multi user ebk.)
1. Metropolitan Museum of Art (New York, N.Y.)—Juvenile literature. 2. Art museums—New York (State)—New York—Juvenile literature. 3. New York (N.Y.)—Buildings, structures, etc.—Juvenile literature. I. Title.
N610.G74 2014
708.147'1--dc23
            2014006384

Printed in North Mankato, Minnesota, in the United States of America
1 2 3 4 5 6 7 8 9 0 18 17 16 15 14

042014
WEP150314

Editor: Heather Kissock
Design: Dean Pickup

Every reasonable effort has been made to trace ownership and to obtain permission to reprint copyright material. The publishers would be pleased to have any errors or omissions brought to their attention so that they may be corrected in subsequent printings.

Weigl acknowledges Getty Images and Alamy as its primary image suppliers for this title.

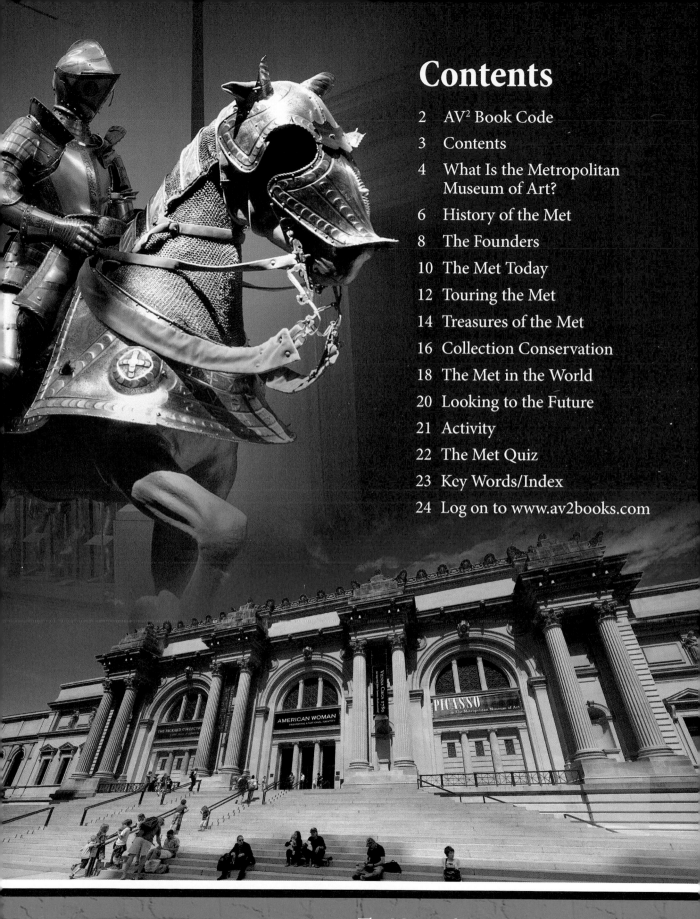

Contents

What Is the Metropolitan Museum of Art?

The Metropolitan Museum of Art is located in New York City. It was founded in 1870 and is the largest art museum in the United States. Work on the new museum began after a group of American business people and artists met in Paris, France. They saw how European museums brought art and education to the people. This group decided to open a museum that would provide Americans with the opportunity to learn about art and art appreciation.

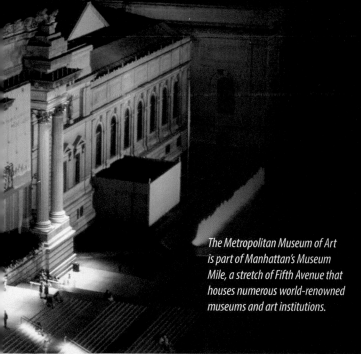

The Metropolitan Museum of Art is housed in two separate buildings. The Main Building is in Central Park. The Cloisters, which is devoted to the art and architecture of **medieval** Europe, is located in northern Manhattan. The Main Building and the Cloisters hold more than two million **artifacts** and works of art. These pieces come from all over the world. The Metropolitan Museum of Art displays its **collection** in more than 17 departments. Each department has its own speciality. The specialties include American art, European paintings, Asian art, Greek and Roman art, and Islamic art. Costumes, musical instruments, and photographs also have separate departments.

The Metropolitan Museum of Art is part of Manhattan's Museum Mile, a stretch of Fifth Avenue that houses numerous world-renowned museums and art institutions.

The Metropolitan Museum of Art is nicknamed

The Met.

More than

400 galleries

are used to display the museum's collection.

The Main Building is

one-quarter of a mile long.
(402 meters)

About

5 million people visit the Met each year.

Almost 70% of these visitors are from other countries.

History of the Met

It was the Fourth of July, 1866. A group of Americans visiting Paris met to celebrate their country's Independence Day. One member of the party, John Jay, began discussing the idea of creating an art gallery for Americans that would be similar to the galleries found in Europe. Jay's words had an impact on the group. Upon returning to the United States, they launched a campaign to gain support for the project. Local leaders, art lovers, and **philanthropists** helped, too. Within four years, they had secured funding for the museum. On April 13, 1870, the Metropolitan Museum of Art opened its doors to the public.

John Jay came from a prominent American family. His grandfather was the first chief justice of the United States.

1880 On March 30, the museum opens at its current location on Fifth Avenue and 82nd Street.

1902 The Met opens its **neo-classical** Fifth Avenue **facade** and Great Hall.

1910 The Metropolitan is the first public museum in the world to buy a piece of art by French painter Henri Matisse.

1875   **1900**   **1925**

1870 The Met opens to the public. Its first home is the Dodworth Building at 681 Fifth Avenue, New York City.

1907 The museum welcomes its first work by French artist Pierre-Auguste Renoir.

The Met's Fifth Avenue facade was designed by architect Richard Morris Hunt. Sculptures were supposed to top the facade's columns, but funding issues halted their progress. The facade remains incomplete even today.

1998 The Arts of Korea gallery opens. It is one of four collections in the Asian department.

2011 The museum opens new galleries for the art of the Arab Lands, Turkey, Iran, Central Asia, and Later South Asia. These galleries include the Met's collection of Islamic art.

1975   2000   2025

2007 The Met completes a major renovation of its Greek and Roman Art galleries. The renovation and reinstallation took 15 years.

2012 The Met completes its renovation of the American Wing and reopens on January 16.

The Founders

Shortly after John Jay returned to the United States, he was appointed to a diplomatic position in Austria-Hungary. He had to leave the planning of the new art gallery to others. A committee was set up to spearhead the project. Artists worked alongside New York's elite to make the art gallery a reality.

John Taylor Johnston (1820–1893)

John Taylor Johnston was the first president of the Metropolitan Museum of Art. Born on April 8, 1820 in New York, Johnston received his early education in Scotland. He later graduated from law school in the United States. Johnston eventually entered the railroad business and became president of the Central Railroad of New Jersey. Johnston was an art collector who owned one of the largest private collections in the country. It was this collection that seeded the Metropolitan Museum of Art.

After retiring as the Met's president in 1889, Johnston was given the title Honorary President for Life.

William Cullen Bryant (1794–1878)

William Cullen Bryant was the first vice-president of the Metropolitan Museum of Art. The son of a surgeon, Bryant was educated in Massachusetts by local scholars. At the age of 21, he was accepted to the bar and began practicing law. His true passion, however, was literature. Already achieving recognition as a poet, Bryant left his law career in 1825 to become an editor in New York. He soon became part of the city's cultural community and played a key role in forming the Metropolitan Museum of Art.

Bryant was the editor-in-chief of the New York Evening Post for 50 years. This position gave him considerable political clout within the city and state of New York.

John Quincy Adams Ward (1830–1910)

John Quincy Adams Ward was an American sculptor. Born in Urbana, Ohio, Ward showed an early interest in art. By the age of 19, he was studying under American sculptor Henry Kirke Brown and later became his assistant. Over time, Ward began receiving his own **commissions**. Several of his sculptures can still be seen on the streets of New York. Known for his realistic bronze sculptures of American subjects, Ward was an early supporter of the Metropolitan Museum of Art. He served on the executive branch of the planning committee.

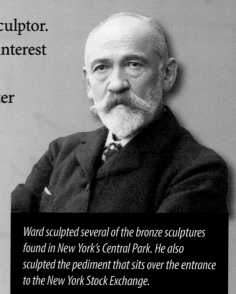

Ward sculpted several of the bronze sculptures found in New York's Central Park. He also sculpted the pediment that sits over the entrance to the New York Stock Exchange.

Frederic Edwin Church (1826–1900)

Frederic Edwin Church was an American landscape painter. Born in Hartford, Connecticut, Church was the son of a wealthy businessman. The family's wealth allowed Church to follow his artistic interests from an early age. After studying under artist Thomas Cole for two years, Church opened a studio in New York City. By the time he was 23, he had been accepted as a member of the National Academy of Design. Initially a painter of local landscapes, Church later became known for his paintings of foreign locales. His stature in New York's artistic community led the Metropolitan Museum to offer him a **trustee**'s position, which he accepted.

Church is the best-known member of the Hudson River School of American painters. This was a group of artists known for their paintings of American landscapes.

The Met Today

The Metropolitan Museum of Art is one of the largest museums in the world. Between the Main Building and the Cloisters, the two locations cover more than two million square feet (185,800 square meters) of space. Its galleries showcase the history of art, from ancient cultures to the modern era. Displaying such a wide scope of art allows the museum to honor the mandate of its founders. To this day, the museum still works hard to provide people with the opportunity to learn about art. In 2000, the museum's trustees added to this original mission. As well as being an institution of learning, the Met is now focused on collecting, preserving, and exhibiting works that demonstrate the pinnacle of human achievement.

The Great Hall is an impressive entrance to the museum. It features three domes, eight archways, a marble floor, and a balcony.

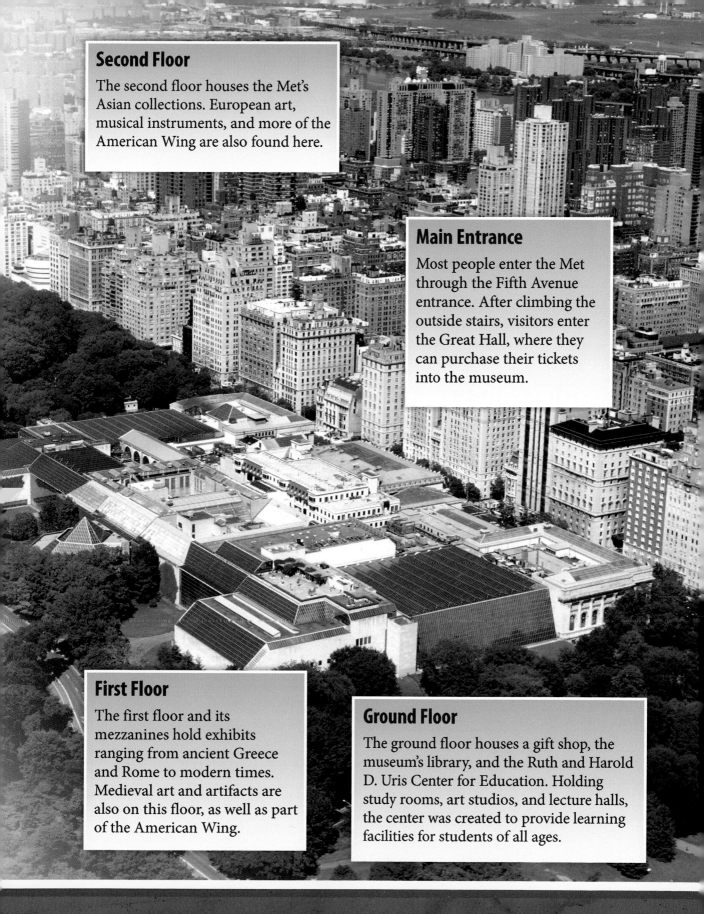

Second Floor

The second floor houses the Met's Asian collections. European art, musical instruments, and more of the American Wing are also found here.

Main Entrance

Most people enter the Met through the Fifth Avenue entrance. After climbing the outside stairs, visitors enter the Great Hall, where they can purchase their tickets into the museum.

First Floor

The first floor and its mezzanines hold exhibits ranging from ancient Greece and Rome to modern times. Medieval art and artifacts are also on this floor, as well as part of the American Wing.

Ground Floor

The ground floor houses a gift shop, the museum's library, and the Ruth and Harold D. Uris Center for Education. Holding study rooms, art studios, and lecture halls, the center was created to provide learning facilities for students of all ages.

Touring the Met

People can spend hours walking through the Met's many galleries. In doing so, they can learn about the artistic history of the United States, as well as countries all over the world. The museum has several key collections that draw visitors year after year.

The American Wing contains the ballroom from Gadsby's Tavern, in Alexandria, Virginia. This ballroom was where President George Washington had his last birthday party.

The American Wing With its most recent renovation completed in 2012, the American Wing provides visitors with more than 30,000 square feet (2,787 sq. m) of American art. Paintings, sculptures, and **decorative arts** from the 18th to 20th centuries are displayed chronologically over two floors of gallery space.

The Sackler Wing The Sackler Wing was built onto the Met's Main Building in 1978 for a specific purpose. The Met had been awarded the right to exhibit the Temple of Dendur, an ancient Egyptian building. Egypt had given the temple to the United States years earlier to thank the country for helping to protect its national treasures. Today, the temple is the centerpiece of the wing.

The Temple of Dendur was built about 15 BC to honor the Egyptian goddess Isis and other Egyptian gods.

The Robert Lehman Wing A set of galleries on the west end of the museum holds European artwork from the 14th to 20th centuries. Donated by banker and art collector Robert Lehman, the collection features 2,600 works, including paintings by such masters as Renoir and Rembrandt, along with sculptures and jewelry.

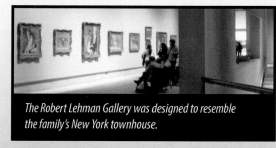

The Robert Lehman Gallery was designed to resemble the family's New York townhouse.

The Cloisters The Met's **satellite** building is devoted to European medieval art and architecture. The Cloisters has about 2,000 works in its collection. The art includes sculptures, **tapestries**, and stained glass.

Located in New York's Fort Tryon Park, the Cloisters contains original architectural elements from medieval structures.

The Met holds the largest collection of

Egyptian artifacts
outside of Egypt.

The American Wing has more than
73 galleries.

Graffiti on the Temple of Dendur dates back
to 10 BC.

Almost 40%
of the people who work at the Met
are volunteers.

The Met is home to the
world's oldest piano,

built in 1720.

1870 The year the Met obtained its first artifact

Out of all the mummy cases on display at the Met, **only 13 contain actual bodies.**

Washington Crossing the Delaware has

the wrong U.S. flag painted on it.

$45 million What the Met spent to purchase a painting by Duccio di Buoninsegna in 2004

29 feet (8.84 m)

The length of the Simonetti carpet, the Met's longest artifact

The Met has at least

9 sphinxes in its collections.

Treasures of the Met

The Met attracts a range of visitors. Some come to the museum to roam the galleries and take a look at all of the collections. Others come to see specific works of art. The Met is an American museum, with works by well-known American artists. It is also a museum of international stature. As such, the Met's collections include works that have meaning to an audience outside the United States.

The Met has an extensive collection of artifacts from ancient civilizations. Visitors from around the world come to see and study these historically important exhibits.

Washington Crossing the Delaware is Leutze's second version of the painting. The first was damaged in a fire.

Washington Crossing the Delaware This life-sized oil painting is one of the Metropolitan's most beloved paintings. It is also one of the most iconic representations of the American Revolution. Created by Emanuel Leutze, the painting shows George Washington's surprise attack against British forces at the Battle of Trenton in 1776.

Madonna and Child This painting was created by Italian artist Berlinghiero in the 1230s. Paintings like this were used to decorate church or home altars. To create its glistening effect, the artist used ground gold in the gold-colored paint. The gold was especially beautiful in candlelight.

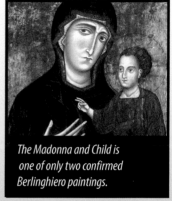
The Madonna and Child is one of only two confirmed Berlinghiero paintings.

The Mangaaka Power Figure was created in the late 19th century in central Africa.

Mangaaka Power Figure A favorite of Met visitors, this statue greets people at the entrance to the African Gallery. Leaning forward, with hands placed on the hips, the figure shows aggression and power. It was designed to make people think about what happens when they break social rules.

Autumn Rhythm Jackson Pollock painted *Autumn Rhythm* in 1950. A work of **abstract expressionism**, it is 17 feet (5 m) wide. To create the work, Pollock poured, dripped, flicked, and splattered thinned paint onto a canvas spread out on the floor. He then moved the paint around with sticks, trowels, and knives.

Even though the paint patterns look random, Pollock planned the form the painting would take.

Collection Conservation

The Met's collection contains works ranging from ancient artifacts to priceless works of art. Taking care of these objects is an important part of the museum's mandate. The Met has a team of **conservators** who focus on this type of work. They evaluate new works acquired by the museum, monitor the art and artifacts already part of the collection, and ensure that all works are being kept in a safe place. Conservators also restore or repair pieces that have been damaged. The Met's conservators work on teams that specialize in specific types of works.

Objects The Objects Conservation team takes care of the museum's three-dimensional artifacts, including sculptures and furniture. Conservators help determine the lighting, **humidity** level, and temperature that each artifact needs to stay in good condition. Besides cleaning the objects, they sometimes have to **fumigate** them as well.

More than 30 people work on the Met's Objects Conservation team.

Paintings The Met's Paintings Conservation Center opened in 1980. It is equipped with tools and equipment needed to assess and repair paintings. High-powered microscopes and x-ray technology allow conservators to study damage, **pigments**, and artistic technique. The information they obtain from this study helps them form treatment plans for the works.

Conservators rely on a number of tools to restore and repair important artworks.

By the time works are put on display at the Met, they have gone through a thorough inspection and have had any necessary repairs made.

Paper and Photography The Center for Works on Paper and Photographic Conservation preserves drawings, prints, and **manuscripts**. Conservators study the physical and chemical nature of the material. This helps them decide the best way to display the artifacts. Some articles are especially fragile. They may need light-tight boxes or specific environmental conditions, such as low humidity or cool temperatures.

Conservators wear gloves when handling artifacts to protect the objects from damage.

Textiles The Textile Conservation department makes the rules for how the museum handles, stores, and displays the tapestries, costumes, and accessories in its collection. To keep textiles from fading, conservators make sure that these artifacts are displayed in dim light. They also take steps to keep people from touching them. Oil and dirt on hands can cause serious damage to the materials over time.

Textile conservators need to know how to weave, spin, sew, and even paint in order to make repairs to this type of artifact.

The Met in the World

As an educational institution, the Met wants to teach as many people as possible about the art in its collections. The museum has programs for people who are able to experience the galleries firsthand. It also has programs for people who are too far away to see the collection in person.

Traveling Exhibits

A key way to extend the Met's reach beyond New York City is through traveling exhibits. **Curators** put together works from the collections and send them on tour to other parts of the world. An exhibit is usually built around a common theme. It may include works by the same artist or be designed around subjects such as nature or a historical era.

The Met hosts traveling exhibits from other museums as well. In 2013, it hosted an exhibit from the British Museum about Ancient Persia.

Educational Programs

Like most museums, the Met has a variety of programs designed to teach people about the art in its collections. Guided tours are available for both schoolchildren and adult visitors. The Met also holds workshops for teachers to help them find creative ways to teach art to their students. Weekly talks, art-making classes, and demonstrations are held throughout the museum to give people the chance to learn more about art.

Children visiting the Met are encouraged to interact with the art through a variety of exercises.

Online Community Access to the Met and its collections is as simple as a keystroke. The Met is active on the internet and has a variety of programs that people can use. Besides having social media accounts, the Met's curators and other staff write a series of blogs that show readers what happens behind the scenes at the Met. The blogs also discuss individual works in the collection, providing descriptions and background information on each piece.

Besides staff, the Met also posts blogs from members of TAG, the museum's Teen Advisory Group. This is open to teens who want to share their views on art.

Travel with the Met The Met encourages people to take an active approach to learning about art. Besides offering tours of its own collections, the Met has a travel program called Travel with the Met. The program allows art lovers to visit galleries and museums around the world. The Met's own staff often lead these trips. This provides guests with an opportunity to see and learn about some of the world's best-known works of art from leading art experts.

Many of the Met's tours take visitors to European locales that are known as cultural and artistic hubs, such as Venice, Italy.

Looking to the Future

The Met is constantly evolving. New exhibits, galleries, and programs help the museum stay current and attract new patrons. Recently, the Met has taken steps to expand its Travel with the Met program. The added adventure travel component provides people with the opportunity to visit remote and lesser-known locations. The excursions include activities such as hiking and outdoor camping.

A newly renovated costume department has also opened. Named after *Vogue* magazine's fashion editor, the Anna Wintour Costume Center houses exhibition galleries, a library, the conservation laboratory, and curatorial offices. Upgrades include a cutting-edge sound system and the latest in projection technology.

The Anna Wintour Costume Center continues the Met tradition of exhibiting fashion from important designers, such as Alexander McQueen.

One of the first Met Adventures tours traveled to Mongolia, where people visited ancient temples and slept under the stars.

Activity

Curators are responsible for organizing exhibitions. They create the theme of the exhibit and plan which works should be included in it. Imagine that you are a curator with the Metropolitan Museum of Art and that you have been given the task of putting together a traveling exhibit that will tour the country.

Use the guidelines below to plan your exhibit.

1. Review the Met's various collections online to decide on a theme for your traveling exhibit. You may decide to base your exhibit on one of the Met's galleries or create a unique theme of your own.

2. Which works in the Met's collections do you feel would best represent your theme? Print copies of the works. On a separate sheet of paper, list each item and make notes that explain why it belongs in your exhibit.

3. Plan the layout of your exhibit. In what order should the works be displayed? Which works should be grouped together? Why?

4. Make a mock-up of your plan by pasting the pictures to a sheet of poster board in the order you want them displayed. Label each work so that people know what they are looking at.

5. Present your exhibit to your friends or classmates. Use your notes to explain the theme of your exhibit and how each of the works fits into this theme.

The Met Quiz

1 Who initiated the plan to build an art institution in New York?

4 Where is the Temple of Dendur displayed?

2 When did the Met open to the public?

5 Name four of the Met's conservation teams.

3 How many pieces of art and artifacts are on display in the Main Building and Cloisters?

ANSWERS:

1. John Jay **2.** April 13, 1870 **3.** More than two million **4.** In the Sackler Wing **5.** Paintings, objects, paper and photography, and textiles.